CGP has Handwriting sorted all autumn!

It's crucial to keep working on Handwriting skills throughout Year 3, and this CGP book is a brilliant way to keep pupils practising regularly...

It's packed with fun, engaging exercises for every day of autumn term, covering all the words they'll need to use most often.

We've included plenty of full sentences and longer pieces to tackle too. — perfect for helping them build up their fluency and confidence!

What CGP is all about

Our sole aim here at CGP is to produce the highest quality books — carefully written, immaculately presented and dangerously close to being funny.

Then we work our socks off to get them out to you — at the cheapest possible prices.

Contents

☑ Use the tick boxes to help keep a record of which pages have been attempted.

Week 1
- ☑ Day 1 1
- ☑ Day 2 2
- ☑ Day 3 3
- ☑ Day 4 4
- ☑ Day 5 5

Week 2
- ☑ Day 1 6
- ☑ Day 2 7
- ☑ Day 3 8
- ☑ Day 4 9
- ☑ Day 5 10

Week 3
- ☑ Day 1 11
- ☑ Day 2 12
- ☑ Day 3 13
- ☑ Day 4 14
- ☑ Day 5 15

Week 4
- ☑ Day 1 16
- ☑ Day 2 17
- ☑ Day 3 18
- ☑ Day 4 19
- ☑ Day 5 20

Week 5
- ☑ Day 1 21
- ☑ Day 2 22
- ☑ Day 3 23
- ☑ Day 4 24
- ☑ Day 5 25

Week 6
- ☑ Day 1 26
- ☑ Day 2 27
- ☑ Day 3 28
- ☑ Day 4 29
- ☑ Day 5 30

Week 7
- ☑ Day 1 31
- ☑ Day 2 32
- ☑ Day 3 33
- ☑ Day 4 34
- ☑ Day 5 35

Week 8
- ☑ Day 1 36
- ☑ Day 2 37
- ☑ Day 3 38
- ☑ Day 4 39
- ☑ Day 5 40

Week 9

- [✓] Day 1 41
- [✓] Day 2 42
- [✓] Day 3 43
- [✓] Day 4 44
- [✓] Day 5 45

Week 10

- [✓] Day 1 46
- [✓] Day 2 47
- [✓] Day 3 48
- [✓] Day 4 49
- [✓] Day 5 50

Week 11

- [✓] Day 1 51
- [✓] Day 2 52
- [✓] Day 3 53
- [✓] Day 4 54
- [✓] Day 5 55

Week 12

- [✓] Day 1 56
- [✓] Day 2 57
- [✓] Day 3 58
- [✓] Day 4 59
- [✓] Day 5 60

Published by CGP

ISBN: 978 1 78908 661 4

Editors: Luke Bennett, Ellen Burton, Eleanor Crabtree, Mary Falkner, Luke Molloy and Hayley Thompson.

With thanks to Camilla Sheridan and Lucy Towle for the proofreading.
With thanks to Emily Smith for the copyright research.

Printed by Elanders Ltd, Newcastle upon Tyne.
Images used on page 5 © www.edu-clips.com
Clipart on the cover and throughout the book from Corel®
Based on the classic CGP style created by Richard Parsons.

Text, design, layout and original illustrations © Coordination Group Publications Ltd. (CGP) 2020
All rights reserved.

Photocopying this book is not permitted, even if you have a CLA licence.
Extra copies are available from CGP with next day delivery • 0800 1712 712 • www.cgpbooks.co.uk

How to Use this Book

- This book contains 60 pages of daily handwriting practice.

- It's split into 12 sections — that's roughly one section for each week of the Year 3 Autumn term.

- A week is made up of 5 pages, so there's one for every school day of the term (Monday — Friday).

- Each page should take about 10 minutes to complete.

- Pupils practise copying individual words, including spelling list words from the National Curriculum, and whole sentences. This helps them to build up their handwriting fluency. Towards the end of the book, they are also given some whole paragraphs to copy.

- A typical page looks something like this:

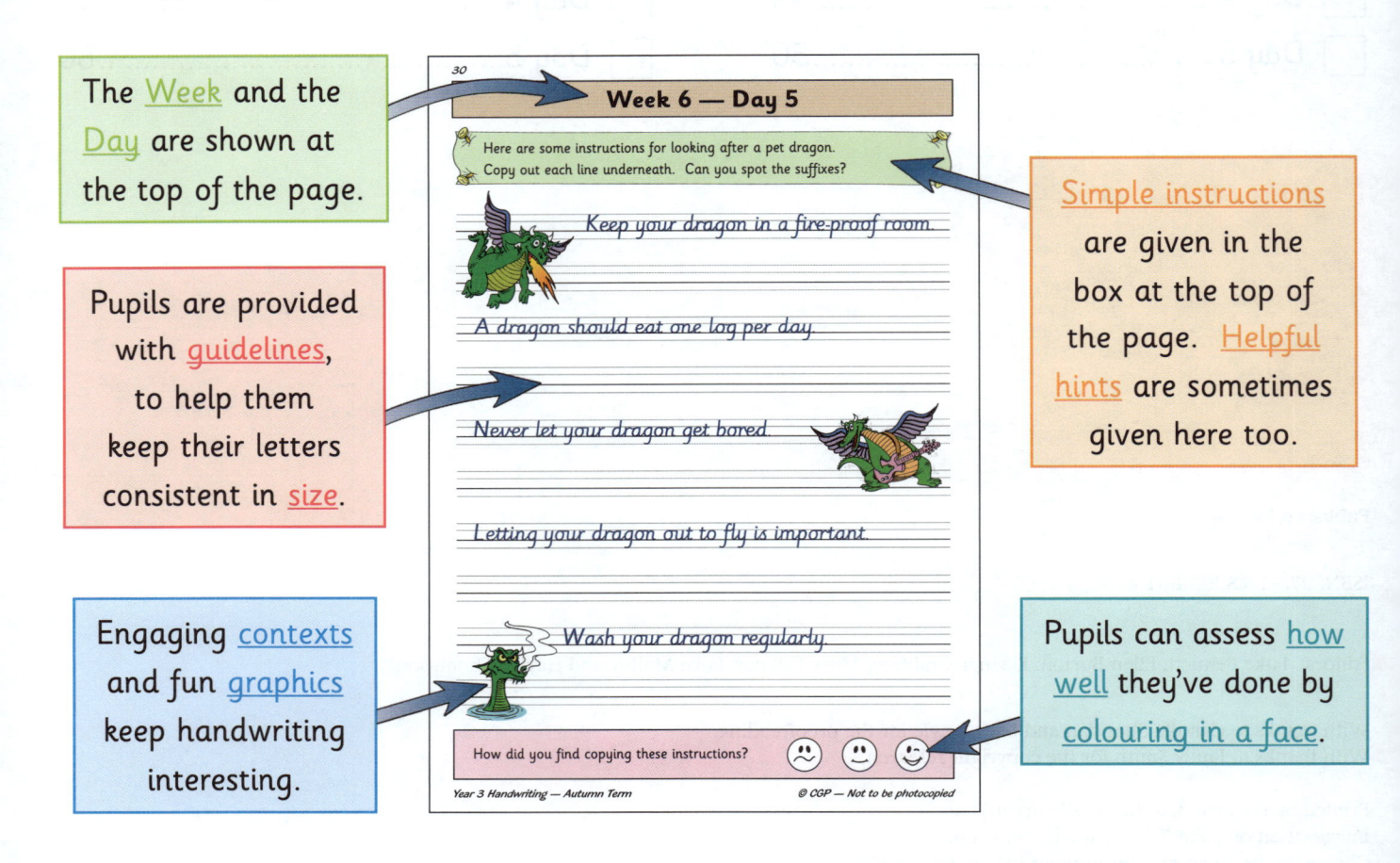

The Week and the Day are shown at the top of the page.

Pupils are provided with guidelines, to help them keep their letters consistent in size.

Engaging contexts and fun graphics keep handwriting interesting.

Simple instructions are given in the box at the top of the page. Helpful hints are sometimes given here too.

Pupils can assess how well they've done by colouring in a face.

If you are a parent or guardian using this book at home with your child, you should bear in mind that different schools have different handwriting styles. You should check with the school to see how they write and join each letter. Some schools also have different break letters (letters that don't join to the next letter). For example, 'g' can be a break letter or can be joined. You should check which break letters the school uses.

Week 1 — Day 1

Here's some practice of the first and second joins. Copy each letter pair three times.

ap

um

iv

ly

ew

it

uf

al

nt

du

hi

kr

mn

aj

mb

ik

ch

ul

il

How did you find the first page of this book?

Week 1 — Day 2

These letter pairs are joined together with either the third or fourth join. Copy each one out three times.

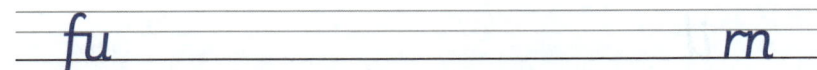

la	do
ms	ad
ig	eq
ac	no
ug	ha
or	rm
wi	op
vy	rv
ow	wy
fu	rn

How did you get on with these letter pairs?

Year 3 Handwriting — Autumn Term

Week 1 — Day 3

Copy out each of these letter pairs three times. They use the fifth or sixth join.

ol

ft

wh

ff

ob

fo

os

wd

oc

ws

rb

of

rk

wk

rf

va

wo

rg

rq

oo

Did you copy all these pairs of letters neatly?

Week 1 — Day 4

Here are some joins to 'e' for you to practise. Copy out each example three times. Then copy the words at the bottom twice.

ne   de

ae   ue

ce   le

he   me

ie   ee

we   te

re

oe   ve

coffee

kettle

How do you think your joins to 'e' went?

Year 3 Handwriting — Autumn Term   © CGP — Not to be photocopied

Week 1 — Day 5

Here are the names of some famous UK places and people. Copy each one out on the lines below it.

Edinburgh Castle

Buckingham Palace

Tower Bridge

Queen Elizabeth II

Joe Wicks

Dame Jessica Ennis-Hill

Sir David Attenborough

Snowdonia

Loch Lomond

How did you get on with these names?

Week 2 — Day 1

These words all have tall letters in them. Copy each one out three times. Use the lines to check your tall letters are the right size.

checked

kitten

third

bubble

hidden

basketball

should

little

diamond

limited

Did you copy these words neatly?

Week 2 — Day 2

These words all have letters with tails in them.
Copy each one out three times.

spray

juicy

energy

copying

jumper

passage

occupy

oxygen

pyjamas

crying

How did you find these words with tails?

Week 2 — Day 3

Here are ten words that have tall letters and letters with tails. Copy each one out three times.

rocky

light

shipwreck

already

jacket

thirty

birthday

pumpkin

pirate

maybe

How did you get on with writing these words?

Year 3 Handwriting — Autumn Term

Week 2 — Day 4

Copy out each of these words three times.
They all contain double letters.

happy

funniest

carrying

ripple

running

pattern

giraffe

puzzle

appear

rabbit

How do you think this page went?

Week 2 — Day 5

This is a poem about a frog. Copy each line out once below it.

A frog hopped out of the bath,

After having a lovely soak.

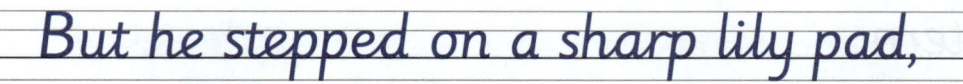

But he stepped on a sharp lily pad,

And let out an almighty croak!

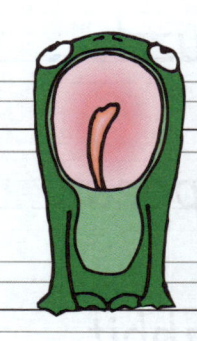

How did you find writing this poem?

Week 3 — Day 1

Try copying out each of these words. Write each one three times.

kind

mind

find

poor

floor

door

behind

child

children

because

Did you write these words neatly?

Week 3 — Day 2

Here are some positive words for you to copy.
They are all adjectives. Try writing each one three times.

pretty

exciting

peaceful

beautiful

amazing

calm

inspiring

wonderful

polite

magnificent

How do you feel this page went?

Week 3 — Day 3

These words are used to describe things negatively.
Practise writing each one three times.

angry

grumpy

scary

worried

untidy

jealous

dishonest

miserable

gloomy

lazy

How did you get on with these negative words?

Week 3 — Day 4

Here are some phrases containing adjectives.
Try copying them out on the lines underneath.

the greedy, fluffy rabbit

an excited, friendly, green dragon

my caring, helpful friend

the orange, musical elephant

her strange, bouncy giraffe

How did you find writing these phrases?

Week 3 — Day 5

Here is a poem about a snake. Copy each line out once below it.

I saw a small, slimy snake,

Eating a really rotten cake.

He took one enormous bite,

Then slowly slithered out of sight.

How neatly did you copy this poem?

Week 4 — Day 1

Practise writing these useful words. Copy each one out three times.

most

break

both

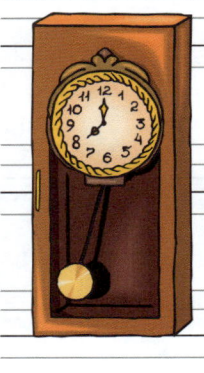

only

hour

every

even

everybody

sure

people

How did you get on with these words?

Year 3 Handwriting — Autumn Term © CGP — Not to be photocopied

Week 4 — Day 2

Here are the names of ten types of animal.
Copy them out on the lines underneath.

platypus

barn owl

emperor penguin

pelican

giant anteater

herring gull

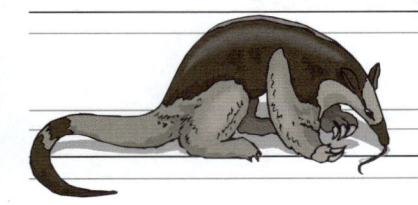

boa constrictor

fallow deer

hippopotamus

rainbow trout

Did you write these animal names neatly?

Week 4 — Day 3

Try copying each of these phrases on the lines below. They are about plants and flowers.

wild strawberries　　*yellow sunflowers*

floating lily pads　　*fields full of daisies*

weeping willow　　*a spiky thistle*

a huge oak tree　　*silver birch*

purple irises　　*a bouquet of red roses*

How did you find this page?

Week 4 — Day 4

Here are some fun facts about animals. Copy each one out neatly underneath. Remember, capital letters don't join to the next letter.

Otters hold hands when they go to sleep.

Some monkeys in Japan make snowballs for fun.

Polar bears have black skin under their white fur.

A group of hedgehogs is called a prickle.

Elephants use mud and sand as sunscreen.

How well did you write these animal facts?

Week 4 — Day 5

Read this story about what it is like to be a zookeeper.
Then copy each line out below it.

This morning, I fed the seals their fish.

I cleaned all the cages and picked up the poo.

Then I got to play with the new baby bear

and give the old tortoise his exercise.

I love my job as a zookeeper!

How did you find this page about a zookeeper?

Week 5 — Day 1

Copy each of these words three times. Remember to use the lines to help you get them the right size.

who

could

should

would

whole

half

many

any

again

after

How did you find writing these words?

Week 5 — Day 2

Here are some places you might find in a town.
Copy each place out on the lines below.

primary school   *theatre*   *library*

post office   *town hall*   *bank*

cinema   *supermarket*   *hairdresser's*

bakery   *pharmacy*

charity shop   *children's playground*

How well did you write these names of places?

Week 5 — Day 3

Here is a shopping list.
Copy out each item from the list once.

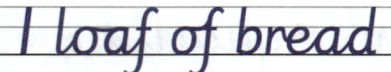

1 loaf of bread

3 pints of milk

6 large potatoes

half a dozen eggs

9 big mushrooms

2 packets of biscuits

4 tins of tomato soup

1 big bag of apples

100 grams of cheese

a bunch of flowers

How did you find writing this shopping list?

Week 5 — Day 4

This page gives some information about a tourist attraction. Copy out each line underneath it.

Visit the Fish Bowl Aquarium.

Come and see the smallest collection of fish ever.

Don't miss your chance to feed the goldfish!

Open Monday to Saturday, 9 am to 4 pm.

£8 for adults, £3 for children, and free for babies.

Did you copy this information neatly?

Week 5 — Day 5

Tracey is staying at a hotel and wants to go to the cinema. She asked at the hotel desk for directions, and the hotel manager wrote a note for her. The note is written below. Copy out each line once.

Turn right when you leave the hotel.

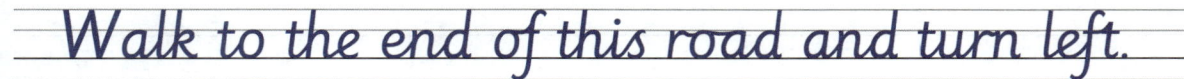

Walk to the end of this road and turn left.

Carry on until you get to the yellow house.

Then turn right. It is at the top of the hill.

I hope you enjoy the film!

How did this page go?

Week 6 — Day 1

Have a go at copying each of these words. Write each one three times.

potatoes

weight

decide

famous

length

medicine

natural

believe

various

island

Could you write each of these words neatly?

Week 6 — Day 2

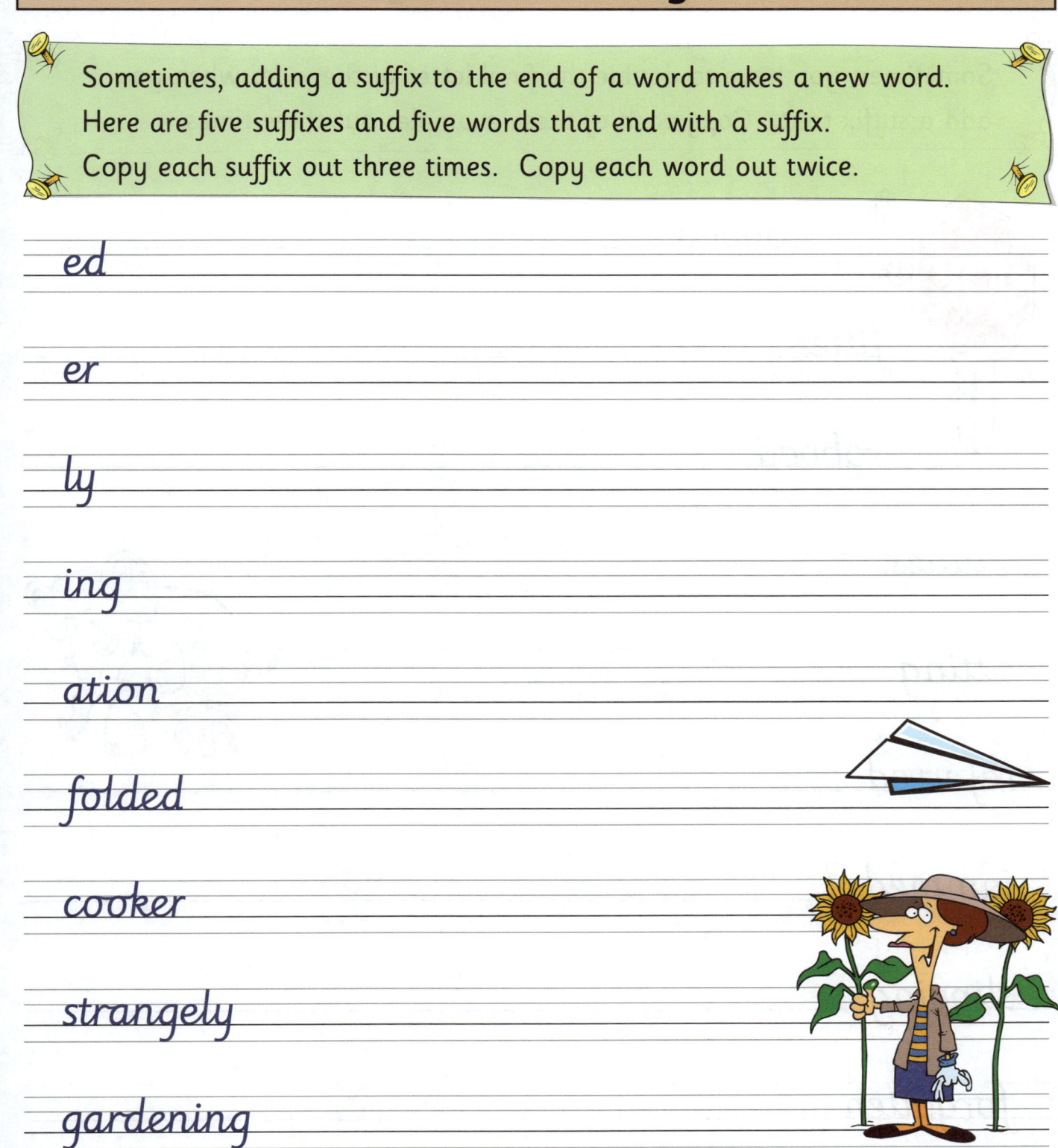

Sometimes, adding a suffix to the end of a word makes a new word. Here are five suffixes and five words that end with a suffix. Copy each suffix out three times. Copy each word out twice.

ed

er

ly

ing

ation

folded

cooker

strangely

gardening

information

How did you do with these suffixes and words?

Week 6 — Day 3

Sometimes, you have to double the final letter of the word when you add a suffix to it. Copy each of these examples out three times.

stopped

fitter

robbed

saddest

sitting

referred

jammed

slipping

forgotten

snorkelling

How well could you write these words?

Week 6 — Day 4

Copy each of these five sentences out on the lines underneath. They all use at least one word with a suffix.

Dev is very good at running.

Nisha quickly passed me the baton.

Dan accidentally dropped the priceless vase.

I had forgotten how much I hate mashed potato.

It was definitely the hottest day this year.

How did you find this page?

Week 6 — Day 5

Here are some instructions for looking after a pet dragon. Copy out each line underneath. Can you spot the suffixes?

Keep your dragon in a fire-proof room.

A dragon should eat one log per day.

Never let your dragon get bored.

Letting your dragon out to fly is important.

Wash your dragon regularly.

How did you find copying these instructions?

Week 7 — Day 1

There are ten words written below. Copy each one three times.

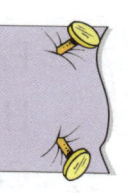

forwards

calendar

sentence

imagine

accident

opposite

bicycle

probably

minute

often

Could you write these words neatly?

Week 7 — Day 2

> Prefixes go at the start of a word to form a new word.
> Here are five prefixes, followed by five words that contain them.
> Copy each prefix three times, then copy each of the words twice.

un

in

dis

mis

im

unhappy

invisible

disconnect

misheard

impossible

How did you find this page?

Year 3 Handwriting — Autumn Term

Week 7 — Day 3

Here are five prefixes and five words containing these prefixes.
Copy each prefix three times, then copy each of the words twice.

re

sub

super

anti

auto

rebuild

subtitles

superstar

antisocial

autopilot

How well did you copy these prefixes and words?

Week 7 — Day 4

Here are five sentences, which all contain a word with a prefix. Copy each one out on the lines underneath.

She had misread the sentence.

I was born with superpowers.

We should retrace our steps back to the castle.

Spinning anticlockwise will break the spell.

I strongly disagree with you.

How did you get on with these sentences?

Week 7 — Day 5

Here is a short news report. Copy it out one line at a time. Don't forget to dot each 'i' and 'j' and put a cross on each 't' when you finish a word.

Police have caught the mystery strawberry thief.

For months, strawberries have been disappearing.

Finally, the culprit has been arrested.

He claimed he had to do it for his jam business.

Police said this was, "not a berry good excuse".

How easy did you find copying this report?

Week 8 — Day 1

Copy out each of these words three times.

thought

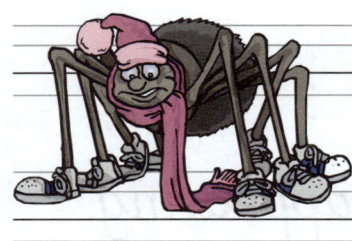

eight

eighth

interest

address

suppose

favourite

remember

enough

quarter

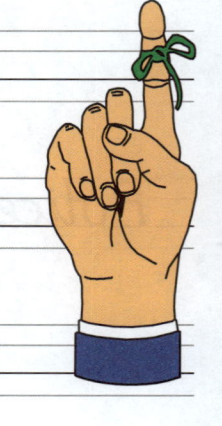

How did you get on with these words?

Week 8 — Day 2

Here is a list of towns and cities in the UK. Copy each one out twice. Remember to make your capital letters reach the top line.

London

Barnsley

Glasgow

Leicester

Warrington

Swansea

Belfast

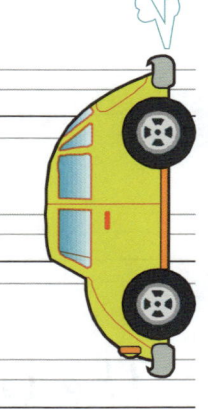

Norwich

Edinburgh

Bangor

How neatly did you write these towns and cities?

Week 8 — Day 3

Here are some facts about the UK.
Copy them out on the lines underneath.

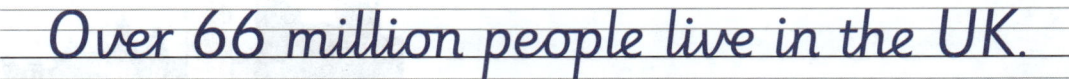

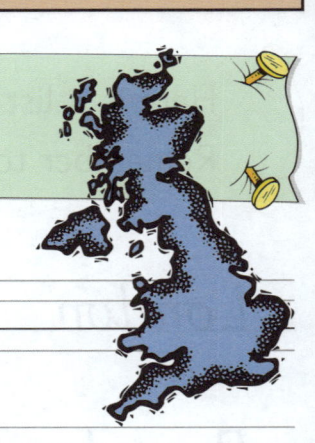

Over 66 million people live in the UK.

The countries in the UK are England, Scotland,

Wales and Northern Ireland.

The UK's Prime Minister lives in Downing Street.

The UK also has a Royal Family.

Do you think you wrote these facts neatly?

39

Week 8 — Day 4

It's time for an adventure... Copy each phrase out once onto the lines below. Try to make all of your small letters the same size.

awesome adventure   treasure chest

brave explorer   ancient map

gloomy cave   long journey

strange creatures   amazing discovery

dense jungle   rickety rope bridge

How do you think this page went?

Week 8 — Day 5

Here are some lines from an adventure story. Copy them out below.

Captain Cassidy had to admit that they were lost.

She had no idea how to get the ship to dry land.

Suddenly the ship jolted, knocking her off her feet.

She looked into the water, and saw something

huge and scaly emerging from the sea.

How did you find copying this story?

Week 9 — Day 1

Copy out each of these words three times.
Try to make the letters and joins as neat as you can.

actual

heard

centre

fruit

actually

promise

busy

pressure

appear

business

Do you think you wrote these words neatly?

Week 9 — Day 2

Homophones are words that sound the same, but they are spelt differently and mean different things. Here are ten pairs of homophones and near homophones. Copy each word once.

ball bawl

here hear

berry bury

meat meet

whose who's

mail male

heel he'll

affect effect

fair fare

grate great

How did you get on with writing these words?

Week 9 — Day 3

Copy out each sentence below. Can you spot the homophones?

He didn't want to meddle in their business.

She deserves a medal for fixing the unicycle.

It feels like it rains all day every day.

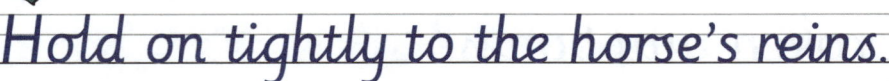

Hold on tightly to the horse's reins.

I am not able to untie this very complicated knot.

Did you write these sentences neatly?

Week 9 — Day 4

> Here are five questions. Copy them out on the lines below. Don't forget to end each one with a question mark.

Where is the nearest trampoline park?

What is the name of your teacher?

Who has eaten the last doughnut?

Have you ever broken any bones?

Why doesn't anyone care about my pigeons?

How well did you copy these questions?

Week 9 — Day 5

Here are some questions and their answers.
Copy them out on the lines below.

What do you like to do at the weekend?

I enjoy going rollerblading most Saturdays.

What are you making for dinner?

I am cooking a spicy vegetable curry.

I am going to serve it with rice and naan bread.

How did you get on with this page?

Week 10 — Day 1

Copy each of these words out three times.

breath

breathe

height

group

exercise

peculiar

experience

build

material

earth

How did you get on with copying these words?

Week 10 — Day 2

Here are ten short phrases, which start with either the word 'a' or the word 'an'. Copy each phrase out once on the lines beneath it.

an old violin			a surprise party

a suspicious rat		a green jumper

a massive pie			an apple tree

an evil vampire			a beautiful morning

a lovely rose garden		an unhappy customer

How well did you copy these phrases?

Week 10 — Day 3

There are five sentences below. Copy each one on the lines underneath.

My mother has a job as a pilot.

The children are reading an interesting book.

We will have a game of tug of war.

It was an accident, I promise.

I would like a new guitar for my birthday.

Did you write out these sentences neatly?

Week 10 — Day 4

Copy each of these sentences about people's hobbies on the lines below.

I go sailing when the weather is nice.

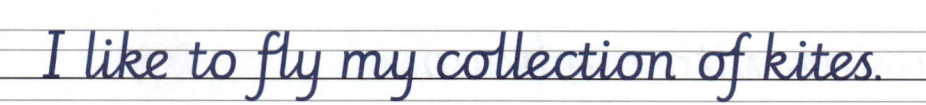

I like to fly my collection of kites.

I go to a chess club once a week.

I enjoy rolling cheese down hills.

My main hobby is painting pictures of ants.

How did you find copying these sentences?

Week 10 — Day 5

An entry from the diary of someone in Year 3 is written below. Have a go at copying the whole thing out in the space underneath.

Today was the first day of half-term. Dad told me to tidy my bedroom this morning, then I played outside with my hoop. After lunch, we looked around the science museum. This evening, we played card games.

Did you copy the diary entry neatly?

Week 11 — Day 1

Copy out each of the words in this list three times.
Remember, when another letter joins to an 's', the 's' tilts slightly.

strength

caught

disappear

continue

question

purpose

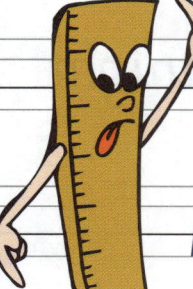

straight

possess

possession

important

How did you get on with these words?

Week 11 — Day 2

Here are some words and phrases that are all to do with time.
Copy each one out underneath.

tonight		yesterday

tomorrow evening		one thousand years ago

last century		next week

every six months		in the next fortnight

two decades		this morning

Could you copy these words and phrases neatly?

Week 11 — Day 3

Here are five facts about Romans in Britain. Copy each one out.

Julius Caesar invaded Britain in 55 BC.

The Romans eventually conquered a lot of Britain.

Romans washed in grand public baths.

They built Londinium, which is now called London.

You can still see Roman ruins in Britain today.

How did you get on with copying these facts?

Week 11 — Day 4

Below is an advert for a time machine.
Copy it out, one line at a time.

Have you ever dreamed of visiting the past?

What about seeing what the future has in store?

If the answer's yes, our time machine is for you!

Travel through time, for just £500 million!

Please remember to time-travel responsibly.

How is your advert looking?

Week 11 — Day 5

Here is a paragraph from a story set during the Second World War. Copy it out in the space below.

Adam's mother sat down with him that evening.

She told him he would be safer from the bombs if he

went to stay with another family in the countryside.

"You can come back to Manchester once this is

over," she said, "but for now, this is for the best."

How did this page go?

Week 12 — Day 1

Copy out each of these words three times. Try to keep them all neat.

century

answer

therefore

extreme

surprise

difficult

experiment

heart

special

perhaps

How neatly do you think you wrote these words?

Week 12 — Day 2

Here are some words and phrases for you to copy out once. They are all related to winter weather.

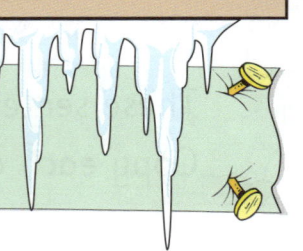

hailstones   wintry rain   blizzard

softly falling snowflakes   icicles

slippery ground   frosty start

frozen puddle   slush   chilly

icy wind   blanket of snow

Brrr... how do you think this page went?

Week 12 — Day 3

These sentences describe a wintry scene. Copy each one out below.

The garden is peaceful after last night's snowfall.

Tree branches are bending with the snow's weight.

A frosty spider's web sparkles in the morning sun.

Birds have left delicate trails of footprints.

The water in the bird bath has frozen.

How did you get on with these sentences?

Week 12 — Day 4

This is a thank you letter that Victoria has written to her Grandma. Copy it out in the space underneath.

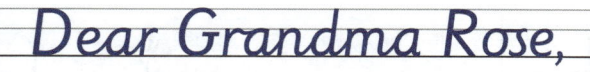

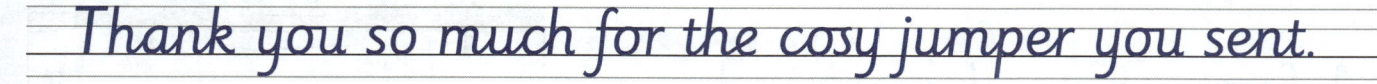

Dear Grandma Rose,

Thank you so much for the cosy jumper you sent.

Red is my favourite colour and it has been perfect

in the cold weather we have been having.

Lots of love from, Victoria

How neatly did you copy this letter?

Week 12 — Day 5

Here is the first verse of a poem called 'Winter-Time', written by Robert Louis Stevenson. Copy it out in the space below.

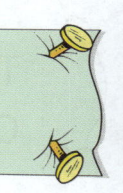

Late lies the wintry sun a-bed,

A frosty, fiery sleepy-head;

Blinks but an hour or two; and then,

A blood-red orange, sets again.

How well do you think you copied this poem?